CHANGING YOUR FINANCIAL DESTINY

A Bankruptcy Attorney Reveals How to Analyze Your Financial
Risk and Make Drastic Changes to Achieve Your Fullest Financial
Destiny

By
David R. Hagen

ISBN 978-0-578-14693-5
Editor: Kirsten Hagen

The information contained in this book is to be considered general legal information only.
It is not intended, nor should it be considered, specific legal advice on any particular
issue. Those with specific questions, or those seeking legal advice which relates to their
specific situation should, of course, seek the advice of a competent local bankruptcy
attorney.

TABLE OF CONTENTS

TABLE OF CONTENTS

I. INTRODUCTION

First and foremost, let me congratulate you for picking up a copy of this book. The Chinese philosopher Lao Tzu once said that "A journey of a thousand miles begins with a single step." Obtaining this book is your first step. This means that you want to achieve your fullest financial destiny.

You may be reading this because you feel hopelessly trapped by debt. You are not alone. In early 2014, the *LA Times* reported that household debt in the United States had recently increased $241 billion to a total of $11.5 trillion. This $11.5 trillion in debt is 9.1% below the peak of $12.7 trillion that occurred just before the Great Recession. However, this is the biggest increase in debt since 2007. This amount is approximately four times the entire yearly budget of the United States Government. Admittedly this includes home mortgages, though it is still an unhealthy amount of debt for American citizens to be carrying. Perhaps you feel you are ready to be free of this crippling financial condition. If so, this book was written for you.

You may be reading this because you feel like you just can't get ahead and save a few dollars. Again, you are not alone. A recent poll by bankrate.com indicated that only 51% of the respondents said that they had more in their rainy day fund than in credit card debt. That is the lowest level since they began doing their survey in 2011. Clearly, this is not good. If you want to learn how to avoid being a part of this group, this book was written for you.

Maybe you have come to the realization that money problems are having an effect on your health or relationships. Half of all marriages in the US end in divorce nowadays and a great many former couples cite financial problems as one of the main causes. If this is the case, this book was written for you.

Whatever financial issues you may be experiencing, this book will help you analyze these issues, fix them, and achieve your fullest financial destiny.

This book is short. It is short for several reasons.

First, most people don't have the time to undertake a complicated financial analysis and implement a complicated plan. In the hustle and bustle of our daily lives, it seems as though we have no extra time. Heck, ask a retired person how their day was and they will tell you how busy they are. This book takes no large time commitment, but it does require some commitment.

Second, I want this advice to be simple. You won't find a lot in this book about stocks and bonds or complicated financial planning. You don't need a degree to make these choices. There are no classes or tapes for me to sell you. These are simple steps I propose and anyone can do on their own or with some advice from a friend. You can always hire someone to give you the fancy advice once you develop some savings.

Third, I want people, including you, to get this done and move forward to a better place in your financial life. If it is too complicated, you won't start it today. The really powerful element of changing you financial destiny involves some long term commitment. Even if you only have ten years till retirement, why would you put off starting your new plan even for one day?

In this book, I am going to give you the benefit of more than thirty years of sitting down with people from all walks of life and discussing, analyzing, and solving their financial problems. We have helped them achieve their fullest financial destiny. I have distilled our experience into this book and come up with a few general principles and guidelines to get you back on track. Give me a couple of hours of quiet reading time and I will lay it all out for you.

II. THE PSYCHOLOGY OF DEBT

You may be feeling some guilt about your current circumstances. Most folks do. The fact that you are feeling guilty is good! It means that you acknowledge some responsibility for your current circumstances. If you were not feeling any guilt regarding your current circumstance, I would question your motives.

Once you have acknowledged that the situation can be analyzed and fixed, you need to put the guilt behind you and develop a plan on how best to proceed.

If a non-bankruptcy solution works for you, the worst that will happen is that you might do some damage to your credit rating or pay some additional taxes.

If bankruptcy is ultimately necessary, it is far from the end of the world. You need to understand that bankruptcy is a constitutional right. The reality that is bankruptcy was discussed among the Founding Fathers when our nation was established. They understood that chronic debt was bad for the fabric of society. Chronic debt creates health problems, family problems and other types of situations. These types of problems have and will drag down society. Accordingly, they borrowed a principle from the Old Testament, which states that money lenders should forgive those who owe them money once every seven years. Certainly there was a lot of wisdom in the ancient law, and the drafters of the Constitution understood this.

It is interesting to note that Thomas Jefferson, who was a brilliant individual and helped create an inspired form of government, was chronically in debt. His estate was also hopelessly mired in debt when he passed away.

If you feel irresponsible, consider the alternative. It's truly irresponsible to not do anything. These problems do not go away by themselves. In fact, I can assure you that the bill collectors will not stop calling. The responsible thing to do is take some action to resolve the issue. If your financial problems are not too severe, it may not even involve filing for bankruptcy. A solution short of bankruptcy may solve your particular problems. However, you should take some action and at least sit down with someone experienced in these matters. Do something today!

One thing we do not get more of in life is time. Don't spend a good deal of it stuck in a financial mess. Take your first step today.

Let's begin.

III. HOW TO REALLY KNOW IF YOU ARE IN FINANCIAL TROUBLE

Getting financial advice and even making the decision to file bankruptcy is a personal one and should only be made on a case-by-case basis. The best way to know for certain whether any action needs to be taken is to talk to a few trusted advisors. A spouse, family member, CPA, minister, or attorney are good choices.

Get two or three opinions on what to do. Different people who see different facets of your life may give you different viewpoints to think about and will ultimately help you arrive at what is best for you.

A friend or family member should be one of your trusted advisors. They know you, your strengths, and your weaknesses. You can trust them.

However, you may also want to sit down with a professional and have them act as one of your advisors. They may not know you as well as a friend, but they will bring valuable experience and objectivity to your analysis.

My suggestion would be to sit down with an attorney or accountant who will charge you a modest fee. There are many bankruptcy attorneys that will not charge for an initial consultation, but there are several reasons you want to be charged a fee. First, you want to be sure that the only thought in the attorney's mind is not that he wants to "sell" you a bankruptcy. Talking you into a bankruptcy is not professional of him or her, but it does happen often. Second, you want to be sure that they are not thinking about unrelated matters like their golf game or next appointment. What I mean by this is if you pay them a small fee, chances are you will have their undivided focus and attention. Third, you want to be sure that they take the time to fully understand your current situation. Now I know a lot of people say they can't afford to pay a professional to meet with them. However, I would suggest that you cannot afford *not* to pay a professional for this important, life changing advice.

For more than thirty years, I have sat down with thousands of people and discussed their financial circumstances. Just when I think that I have seen or heard it all, someone comes along with another unique problem which needs to be solved. About 50% of the people that I have met with filed bankruptcy. However, perhaps more importantly, the other 50% did not. We were able to come up with an alternative solution that solved their problem short of bankruptcy.

During this time, I developed some basic criteria to determine whether someone is really in trouble and perhaps even needs to file a bankruptcy.

1. Negative Cash Flow

If you are spending more than you make each month, this is a warning sign that some type of corrective action must be taken. This is called negative cash flow. Negative cash flow, even if only for a few months, can cause financial ruin. Something needs to be done to correct the situation at once. Quite simply, expenses must decrease or income must increase.

There are many reasons for this: illness, divorce, loss of job, or poor money management. Notice that three of these four causes are situations that are not usually anticipated. That is, most people don't even see an illness, a job loss, or a divorce coming. Poor money management often times is a much smaller, more difficult, issue to detect until a family slips very slowly and gets in over their head.

In fact, Wall Street almost encourages us to have negative cash flow because they are always trying to sell us a product with the next commercial. Sometimes they use the most insane arguments or scenarios in an attempt to get us to buy. Being human beings, we are naturally susceptible to this kind of advertising and easily fall into their negative cash flow trap.

The easiest place to finance negative cash flow is on credit cards. However, credit cards are usually the last place anyone wants to finance monthly negative cash flow. Credit cards are essentially high interest loans. Yes, it might be easy or even prestigious to use a credit card but if the balance is not being paid off on a monthly basis it is very dangerous trap. Big card companies really don't care if it is a risky investment so long as you are able to manage your cash flow and make your payments on time. They couldn't care less that your cash flow is negative or that your debts far exceed your assets. They just want you to continue to pay in on their high-end interest loan. This is a very lucrative business for them. If it was not, they wouldn't have every other expensive ad playing during the Super Bowl!

If you look at your finances and your cash flow is negative or you can't find a way to fix it within six to twelve months, you will have a problem. Again, you either need to increase income or decrease expenses. It's that simple. The difficult part is to have a system in place so you can effectively evaluate your cash flow and then force yourself to take some time to actually look at this data so you can understand the big picture.

I am continually amazed at how many people I meet with have no idea whether their cash flow is positive or negative each month. Someone that doesn't know their cash flow is usually heading for a problem unless they are incredibly wealthy. Fortunately, it only takes about three to five minutes of questions that I have developed over the years to determine within several hundred dollars whether they are cash flow even, negative, or positive.

If you don't know whether your cash flow is even, negative, or positive and you feel like you don't have enough money left over to put something into savings at the end of the month, chances are you probably have a negative cash flow. The first thing that you need to do to fix this is buy a program, like Quicken for example, and set up some charts of accounts based upon the money you spend each month. You can get this data from your checkbook, your bank statement and your credit card statement. Be sure to try to account for what you spend your cash on as well. Then take a look at your income and your expenses from month to month. I think that most people would be shocked at how much they spend on different necessities for everyday life. For example, most people spend a great deal of their income on eating out. Gifts for others are another area that tends to catch people by surprise.

I also see folks spending an exorbitant amount on their vehicle. For example, experts recommend that you should not spend more than 10% of your net income on your transportation expense. This includes car payment, gasoline, repairs, and registration. I have met with people that pay more for their vehicle then most people pay for their mortgage! Those who spend too much on their vehicle are putting themselves at a great disadvantage financially. They need to make some dramatic changes if they want to achieve their fullest financial destiny.

The bottom line here is that you need to know exactly what you make and spend each month. If you don't, you could be hiding from trouble. Once you know your flow, you can analyze it and see if there is a problem that needs to be corrected. If your cash flow is negative act fast, and certainly don't finance negative cash flow on credit cards as this is usually financial suicide.

2. You owe more than you make in a year

If you owe more than one year's salary (before taxes) to unsecured creditors (credit cards, personal loans, judgments, etc.), this is a sign that you're in trouble. Too large a portion of your monthly income will need to be used to service this debt.

Something, potentially even bankruptcy, must be done to remedy this problem.

These problems will only get worse. The interest rate on your debt will cause that sum to double every few years. For example, if you are only paying 10% average on your credit cards, your debt will double in seven years. This is simple math. Think how fast this debt will double if you are paying an average of 21%. If your debt is equal to six months of your annual salary and you are paying 21% you will be financially terminal in less than four years if you do not act. Your debt will double and you will then owe what you make in a year, causing you to be stuck in a corner. If you don't have assets to sell, your only remedy might be bankruptcy. Don't let this happen to you. I will discuss how to use this math to your advantage later in this book in Chapter 9.

Simply paying the minimum monthly payment on your cards is a fool's game. Depending on your interest rate, paying off your balance by paying the minimum monthly payment can take as long as twenty-seven years. Who would knowingly do this? Again, this is great business for the credit card companies, even when they know that about 4% of these balances will go away due to their customers filing bankruptcy. If it were legal, wouldn't you loan money to someone at 21% even while knowing that 4% of the principal would not come back to you?

You bet you would! This is great business for them and seeing that we live in a free country, they can pretty much do what they want. You just have to learn to be smarter than them and protect your financial health.

3. Your financial situation is affecting your health or relationships

I have seen many people whose health has deteriorated from worrying over their financial issues. Many who suffer from monetary struggles are taking antidepressants or other drugs to treat issues that result from stress. I remember one woman who came in for a consultation who was so stressed out that she broke down weeping every few minutes. Unfortunately, I have even had a few clients actually commit suicide. They simply could not let go of the guilt they harbored over their finances. Obviously, someone who kills themselves over debt have some value issues. But what this does emphasize is that debt is a serious issue. I remember one woman who was dying of cancer and had been told by her doctor to get her affairs in order. After the bankruptcy was filed, I was amazed to learn that her cancer went into remission. It is truly amazing what our mental health can do for our physical health.

I have consulted with many couples who wanted to deal with their debt first and then get divorced. As I have already said, financial problems and marital problems seem to go hand in hand. For most of these couples, when I inquired whether they still wanted a divorce attorney referral at the end of the bankruptcy, I am not surprised when they indicate that many of their marital problems had worked themselves out now that the pressure of their debt was resolved.

Think about it this way, are family and health more important than money? Of course they are. Anyone who sits down and thinks about it for a bit will tell you this. When someone looks at the big picture, the answer is clear. Yet, most people don't see the insidious effect of debt in their lives until it has already done the damage. Don't let this happen to you. Make the effort to look at the bigger picture.

4. Judgments

A judgment results when someone files a lawsuit against you. If you don't respond or if you go to trial and lose, the court will then enter a judgment against you for a specified amount. Each state differs on how a person can enforce a judgment against someone. However, common methods are wage garnishment, bank levy, picking up personal property such as vehicles, or putting a lien on a home.

To me, a judgment is a sign that something has gotten out of control. It is an easy yellow flag to spot. Judgments are usually so disruptive to a person's financial life that they are many times the final straw that puts a person with marginal finances into a critical situation where bankruptcy starts to look like a viable alternative.

Now, none of these four criteria are conclusive. That is, these are just issues to consider when deciding whether you have serious financial problems. Don't think that if you are experiencing two out of four that you are in serious financial trouble. Rather, these are things to think about and consider as you discuss your financial situation with your trusted advisors.

Let me give you a few examples:

I remember one time I sat down with a young lady who worked in a fast food restaurant. She made about $900 a month after tax (this was many years ago). Though not lazy, earning $900 a month as an assistant manager was the greatest utility of the skills that she had. Somehow, she had let a creditor get a judgment against her for $4,000. This creditor was garnishing her wages and took 25%

of what she made. She was barely making it on $900 a month as is, but she certainly wouldn't be able to make it on 75% of that amount. In California, a creditor can garnish your wages, but only up to 25%. She wanted to file bankruptcy in the worst way. As you can see from my criteria above, she probably only fell into one of the four general criteria. Nonetheless, she certainly did need help. I talked her out of filing the bankruptcy and got permission from her to call the creditor. I offered them my full fee in satisfaction of the debt. The creditor indicated that would not be sufficient because they were extremely good at exacting money from those who had judgments against them. We then promptly filed her bankruptcy proceeding. The story has a happy ending in which she received a discharge of this debt and went on to live a very successful and happy life. However, it is unfortunate that the creditor did not look at the big picture and agree to take something as opposed to nothing for his client.

Another extreme example would be someone who I saw who made $100,000 per year gross income but had several hundred thousand dollars in debt. Clearly, his annual income was much less than his debt. Sounds like an easy analysis, right? Not necessarily. This person also had some unique assets that would be lost in a bankruptcy proceeding. He got acting residual payments (payment for a prior acting job) totaling more than $100,000 per year. These residual rights would be lost in a bankruptcy proceeding. So even though he had trouble, bankruptcy was not a good solution for him even though the debt was significantly higher than his annual income. After a long conversation, we came up with two or three other ways to handle this debt short of filing a bankruptcy.

Every couple of months, I sit with someone who has sufficient income and even assets, yet has a large amount of debt. They want to file bankruptcy or do something less dramatic to fix the problem. After a long conversation, we realize that they simply are experiencing money management problems or simply spending too much on something that can be curtailed (like eating out or traveling). I remember one time I sat down with a very successful attorney friend who was concerned that he may need to file bankruptcy. After a conversation, it turned out that he didn't really meet any of the criteria above. Sure, he had debt that had built up, but I could not tell what the source of the debt might be. It turns out that he really didn't know what he was making or spending each month. No one was taking care of the management of his law firm nor paying the bills in a timely manner. We recommended that he immediately bring in a part time bookkeeper for only half a day per week. What he found out was amazing. The bookkeeper found out that the firm was actually pretty profitable if the bills were simply paid on time and they avoided all the late fees that were being paid. Giving his cash flow the extra pair of eyes completely solved the problem. There are so many ways that folks just get turned upside down by various financial issues, both large and small. Because we don't focus on them, things can get really out of control fast.

The point I'm trying to make is that the above criteria are something to consider, but the only way to really tackle these issues is to gather up some information and sit down with one or two of your trusted advisors.

IV. SOLUTIONS

Over the years, I have developed several common solutions to serious financial problems. People should consider all these solutions if they determine that they have severe financial troubles. Notice that the first three options are not bankruptcy solutions. This is as it should be. Bankruptcy, while a powerful and effective solution, should always be among the last choices. There are some down sides to bankruptcy which I will discuss later in Chapter 7. Again, half of a thousand people and businesses I have consulted with over the years did not need to ultimately file bankruptcy. Here are the most common solutions to debt.

1. Borrow money from a bank at a lower interest rate to retire high interest credit cards

It seems like this would be an obvious solution to someone not actually wrapped up in a difficult financial situation. Most credit cards carry interest rates of 21% or more. It certainly would make sense to borrow money from a bank at 10% to pay off debt that is bearing interest at the rate of 21%. As I said before, if someone is making minimum money payments on a 21% interest credit card, it will take them as much as twenty-seven years to fully retire the debt. A 10 year bank loan at a lower interest rate would turn a financially terminal into a potentially viable financial circumstance.

The problem with this plan of action is banks are very hesitant to make unsecured loans. The reason behind this is after the loan is made the borrower can then turn around and file a Chapter 7 bankruptcy. While this seems like an obvious and first choice for everybody many times it is not a practical solution.

Now if a person has collateral, like a house, a bank may make a loan if there is sufficient equity in the property to either get a second loan on the property or refinance with a slightly larger first. This money can then be used to pay off the debt that is gathering 21% interest and doubling every 4 years to a lower interest rate and into a loan that can be paid off over many, many years. Debts that were costing a total of $1,000 per month in minimum payments can be shifted to a mortgage that will increase perhaps only $400 per month. This makes some sense to me in certain circumstances.

When real estate went up in value so quickly in the early 2000s, we sent many folks to mortgage brokers to consider a refinance of their property. If they made sure that their new loan contained no surprises and took steps to prevent debt from building up again, they were a success story. Unfortunately, some took out more than they needed and didn't take any time to look at the fine print in the new loan. (Also, many were apparently deceived by the brokers or their banks). In any event, when done properly, this is a very effective remedy to a debt problem. Be sure to read the fine print and know what you're getting into.

2. Sell assets and pay debt

If a person has enough equity in assets, they can sell them and pay off the debt. For example, I met with someone that had $20,000 in high interest credit card debt. They also had a car they owned free and clear that had a value of approximately $20,000. I suggested that they sell the vehicle, even though they loved it dearly, to pay the debt. If they needed a car to get around I suggested that they buy or lease another vehicle that had a much smaller monthly payment. Again, while this solution may seem obvious, it is difficult for people who are directly wrapped up in financial problems to sometimes see it as a solution. Again, don't be afraid to look at the bigger picture.

Now this same person could have borrowed some money and used the car as collateral. Sometimes these are call "car title loans." We seem to see these much more often these days. Why do you think this is? The answer is because it is very good business for the lender. Unfortunately, the borrower is usually someone that can least afford this type of debt.

I saw a car title loan that had an interest rate of 84%. If someone is truly in dire need of taking care of their loans, they are far better off to sell the car, pay the debt, and then buy a car of lesser value for a while or sell the car and lease another with affordable monthly payments.

Car title loans are almost always a losing proposition.

3. Settle debt

People who have old debt can call creditors and try to settle. If an account is significantly past due, a creditor understands that the person may be contemplating bankruptcy or simply may not have the ability to repay. These creditors will often settle for a lump sum settlement. Many times they will settle for a much smaller amount. However, some creditors will fixate on receiving a settlement of 80% or more. I tell clients that any pool of delinquent debt, with various accounts in it, will settle for approximately 50%. Put together a small amount of cash and settle the accounts one at a time. When doing this, a person can do it themselves or through an attorney. However, you must be very sure that it is clear with the creditor that the debt is considered satisfied upon receipt of the lump sum settlement. This should be in writing every time.

Of course, if a person does not have some funds with which to settle the debt or does not have income within which to pool up some money to settle the debt, this alternative may not be viable. Further, you should check with your tax advisor to see if settling debt might cause your tax burden to increase as a result.

4. Chapter 13 Bankruptcy

Chapter 13 permits you to pay your creditors in monthly installments over three to five years. A formal plan is prepared which allocates how much money will be paid to your creditors each month. This plan is submitted to the Bankruptcy Court and the Chapter 13 Trustee for approval.

To qualify for Chapter 13, your unsecured debts must be less than $336,900 and your secured debts must be less than $1,010,650. These numbers increase every few years but are accurate as of 2014.

Chapter 13 is most often used when there would be some problem with filing a Chapter 7 bankruptcy. For example, if your mortgage payments are behind and you do not have the ability to bring the payments current in the next few months, you will want to consider Chapter 13. It allows the past due payments to be paid in installments over 36-60 months. However, mortgage payments that are due after the filing of the Chapter 13 must be kept current or the bankruptcy will be dismissed. Chapter 13 will not work if you cannot keep the trust deed current *and* make the monthly plan payments.

If you have considerable assets which could be lost in a Chapter 7, you might consider filing Chapter 13. Chapter 13 permits you to keep all your assets, even if their value exceeds the amount of the allowed exemptions. Exemptions are discussed later in Appendix A. The reason you can keep these assets is that over time you will be paying your creditors the value of these assets.

Some debts that may not be discharged in Chapter 7 can be made to go away with a Chapter 13. For example, community property equalization payments arising out of a divorce are not dischargeable in Chapter 7. However, they can be discharged in Chapter 13.

If your monthly income is greatly in excess of your monthly expenses, you may need to file a Chapter 13 bankruptcy. The Court will not allow you to file a Chapter 7 if your income significantly exceeds expenses.

Lastly, taxes which are not dischargeable can be repaid over a three-to-five year period while under the protection of the Bankruptcy Court.

There are at least two hearings in every Chapter 13 Bankruptcy. The first is called the "First Meeting of Creditors" in a 341(a) hearing. This is before a Chapter 13 Trustee where you discuss your assets, liabilities, amenities, and expenses. The second is called a "Confirmation Hearing" that is before your Judge and where your repayment plan is submitted and, hopefully, approved by the Court.

5. Chapter 11 Bankruptcy

Chapter 11 also reorganizes debts by submitting a repayment plan to the court. This chapter is used when debts exceed the dollar limits of a Chapter 13 discussed above. Chapter 11 is more complex and expensive but does offer greater flexibility. Businesses usually file under Chapter 11.

Annually there are many hearings before a Trustee and the court in various issues in Chapter 11.

This type of bankruptcy requires extensive accounting reports and records which must be submitted to the Office of the United States Trustee during the bankruptcy.

6. Chapter 7 Bankruptcy

Chapter 7 is often referred to as "straight" bankruptcy and is by far the most common. All exempt assets are retained by you, free from creditors' claims except mortgages and other secured debts. Assets that cannot be exempted are sold and the proceeds divided among your creditors. Your debts are then discharged, meaning legally terminated, and you are free to start your financial life anew.

By far, the vast amounts of bankruptcy filings in the US every year (about 85%) are Chapter 7 proceedings.

In most cases, there is only one hearing in Chapter 7 before a bankruptcy Trustee. Many times, it will last less than a few minutes.

Sometimes we will even use a combination of two or more solutions to solve a person's problem. For example, if a person can sell assets, but not pay off all their debt, we may follow the sale with some debt settlement. Or, if a person sells an asset and pays taxes that will not discharge in a bankruptcy, we can later file a Chapter 7 bankruptcy to get rid of the rest of the debt. There is not one solution for every problem. Rather, a custom solution should be crafted for each person or couple.

V. PICK YOUR PATH AND DEVELOP YOUR PLAN

After analyzing your issues with your advisors, it is time to pick your path. Choose which is best for you. I want you to write this path down in the top of a single piece of paper. Next, you need to develop your plan. Write down all the things you and your advisor can think you need to do to implement the plan. Again, do this on a single sheet of paper. Don't make this more complicated than it needs to be. You need simplicity and clarity to carry out your new plan. It should be so simple that you could almost recite it from memory. If it is too complex, you will get lost.

The next thing you need to do is take the first step on your list. You should do this now.

Today.

Right now.

Clients seem to tell me the same three or four things over the years in almost every bankruptcy proceeding. One thing they tell me is that their only regret going through a bankruptcy proceeding is that they waited too long. Do not wait too long to put in place a financial solution, even if it is not a bankruptcy proceeding. Do the analysis, choose the solution, and proceed. Do it now.

VI. EXEMPTIONS

If bankruptcy is a consideration, you need to know what assets may be lost in exchange for getting a discharge of your debts.

State exemption laws are designed to protect certain items of property from execution by judgment creditors or the Bankruptcy Court if a debtor files for protection under the Bankruptcy Code. The law has its genesis in the English Common Law which did not allow for creditors to take a debtor's clothing. This law was not necessarily designed to protect debtors, but to avoid breaches of the peace caused by naked debtors wandering the streets!

The California Constitution requires the state legislature to provide an exemption scheme to protect individuals from the "extreme consequences of economic misfortune "[California Constitution Article 20, § 1.5]. Accordingly, California has a statutory scheme whereby debtors are allowed to protect certain items of their possession to assist them in their "fresh start."

The California legislature has enacted a dual system whereby a debtor can choose one of two sets of exemptions. The selection of which set of exemptions to use should be done with the help of a

Bankruptcy attorney. However, a debtor cannot use exemptions from each set of exemptions. They must opt for one set or the other and the set of exemptions used will generally depend upon the nature and extent of a debtor's assets. Further, joint debtors (generally a husband and wife) are not entitled to two sets of exemptions. They must elect one set of exemptions as a couple.

The Bankruptcy Code provides that, to be eligible to claim a particular state's exemptions, a debtor must reside in that state for 2 years preceding the bankruptcy filing. If they did not reside in any one state for that period, then the laws of the state in which they resided during the 180-day period before the 2-year period applies (or during a longer portion of the 180-day period than in any other place). If this sounds confusing, it is. Courts and attorneys around the country are struggling to deal with the interpretation of these new Code provisions.

A list of both sets of exemption lists are shown in Appendix A at the end of this book.

VII. NON-DISCHARGEABLE DEBT

If bankruptcy is a consideration, you need to know what debts might not be discharged. Examples of debts that may not be discharged in bankruptcy are:

1. Debts incurred shortly before filing bankruptcy

   Debts incurred within 60 days of filing the bankruptcy for "luxury goods or services" are not dischargeable. "Luxury goods or services" can include any type of spending for "non-essentials" which might appear inappropriate considering your current financial circumstances. Cash advances obtained within 60 days of the bankruptcy filing are not dischargeable. Also, incurring debts at any time which you knew, or should have known, you could not pay constitutes fraud. It is improper to incur debt when you know you cannot repay the debt or that you are going to file bankruptcy. These debts can be held nondischargeable.

2. Taxes

   (a.) Income Taxes

Taxes owed to the United States or any state, county, or other governmental entity are normally nondischargeable. However, income taxes will discharge if all of the following criteria are met:

(1) the taxes are more than three years old at the time the bankruptcy was filed. (The three-year period begins to run from the time the returns were due, plus any periods of extension.);

(2) if the return was not filed on time, more than two years has expired since the return was filed;

(3) if there was an assessment, more than 240 days have expired from the date of the assessment;

(4) there is no lien on any property which you own;

(5) there has been no fraud.

(b.) Employment Taxes

(1) Trust Fund Taxes

A trust fund tax includes income taxes which an employer is required to withhold from the pay of his or her employees, the employees' share of social security and railroad retirement taxes, and also federal unemployment insurance. Trust fund taxes are never dischargeable.

(2) Employer's taxes

An employment tax is the employer's contribution required to be paid in addition to the amount withheld from the employee's paycheck. An employment tax is dischargeable provided the date the last return was due, including extensions, is within three years before the filing date.

(c.) Excise taxes

Excise taxes include sales taxes (in some states), estate and gift taxes, gasoline taxes, and other federal, state or local taxes. To be dischargeable, the transaction giving rise to the tax must have occurred more than three years before the filing of the petition. If a return needs to be filed, three years must have elapsed since the return was due, including any extensions.

(d.) Sales taxes

The Bankruptcy Code does not specifically address the dischargeability of sales taxes. In California and Hawaii, excise taxes are imposed on the retailer for the privilege of doing business. Thus, sales tax in these states appear to be more of an excise tax and are dischargeable if more than three years have elapsed from the filing of the return, or if no return is necessary, three years from the date of transaction give rise to the tax.

(e.) Property taxes

Property taxes assessed and payable within one year before the petition is filed are nondischargeable.

Disclaimer: Discharging taxes is an extremely complex analysis. There are many exceptions to these general rules. You should have these be done utilizing a bankruptcy attorney and your accountant.

3. Support payments

Alimony and child support are not dischargeable in bankruptcy. Support obligations created by a Family Law Judgment are nondischargeable.

4. Wrongful acts

Liabilities arising from a wrongful act, such as a judgment for fraud, assault, conversion, or embezzlement, can be held nondischargeable.

5. Wages

Wages owed to others and which were incurred within three months prior to the bankruptcy can be held nondischargeable.

6. Penalties or fines

A penalty or fine, usually assessed by a Court or the Government, is nondischargeable. Traffic tickets won't go away!

7. Student loans

In October 1998, then-President Clinton signed the Higher Education Amendments Act of 1998. It provides that all student loans, regardless of age, are nondischargable. This replaces the seven-year requirement which had been in effect for many years.

The Bankruptcy Code provides a limited exemption for "undue hardship". The ninth Circuit has adopted a formal test to determine whether a student loan could be discharged due to undue hardship. A debtor must show: (1) that they cannot maintain, based on current income and expenses, a minimal standard of living for themselves and their dependents if forced to pay the loans, (2) that additional circumstances exist indicating that this state of affairs is likely to persist for a significant portion of the repayment of the student loan, and (3) that they have made a good faith effort to repay the loans.

Getting a discharge due to an undue hardship is very fact-intensive and involves filing a lawsuit against the lender and ultimately a trial. It should only be done with an attorney.

Furthermore, the courts have been reluctant to grant an undue hardship discharge unless a person is in very bad shape.

8. Debts incurred in connection with a divorce

Any debt incurred in connection with a divorce or separation, which is payable to the ex-spouse, is nondischargeable in a Chapter 7 filing. This usually applies to obligations to a former spouse to equalize the division of community property. It may also apply to other obligations such as the obligation to hold a former spouse harmless on debts or to pay his or her attorney's fees. If you have any debts such as this, you should discuss them with your attorney before the bankruptcy is filed and show them the dissolution documents.

9. Secured debts

Bankruptcy will not discharge debts that are "secured." Secured debts are where you pledged some type of collateral to ensure the repayment of a debt. Obviously, a bankruptcy would not allow you to stop making payments on your car and still keep the vehicle. The same holds true with "purchase money security interests" on household goods. If you pledged a refrigerator or a sofa as collateral for the repayment of a debt, you cannot keep the item and not make the payments. However, you do have the option to return the item and pay nothing. This decision is yours to make. When a situation such as this arises, consult us. We will advise you on what to do. Many times, it can be arranged so that you can keep the item and make payments at a reduced rate. Each retailer handles their security interests differently so it is important that your rely on our experience to guide you through this area.

VIII. DISADVANTAGES OF BANKRUPTCY

The advantages to bankruptcy seem so significant in the right situation. There are, however, some disadvantages to bankruptcy which must be taken into consideration.

First, a bankruptcy filing can remain on your credit report from seven to ten years. While this is something to consider, most clients find that it is not insurmountable. Many clients are surprised to receive new credit within a few years after they filed bankruptcy.

Second, you cannot file another Chapter 7 bankruptcy for eight years. While this means that you give up your financial "safety net" for this period of time, few people require a second bankruptcy. If additional problems arise, you may still file a Chapter 13 bankruptcy any time after the Chapter 7 proceeding is concluded.

Third, it may be difficult to purchase a home or rent a new apartment for a few years. Real estate brokers and lenders tell us that after these few years following your bankruptcy buyers can qualify for real estate loans once again. This is especially true if they have a sizeable down payment and a good payment history after the bankruptcy.

As you can see, there are some negatives to consider when contemplating bankruptcy. However, they might be quite small if the amount of debt to be discharged is significant.

IX. STARTING FRESH

Once someone achieves their goal of being at a breakeven point, the next step is putting the plan in place to move ahead in a very thoughtful, purposeful, and beneficial way. Otherwise, someone has simply wasted the opportunity.

It seems to me that a lot is made of financial planning and that it get complex very fast. It gets so complex that it causes people to not even set up a plan.

I want to present to you a much simpler way to go about this:
  -Set some goals
  -Create a plan to achieve these goals and
  -Regularly follow up

Set aside a time in the next few days to go off alone with a pad of paper. Write down what you would like to achieve in the next year. Really dream about what would make you happy. The list should contain financial goals, but also personal goals such as lifestyle, family, and even spiritual goals. Be realistic. I would love to play scratch golf, work fewer hours and run for political office, but I try to be honest with myself when I set goals. You don't need much detail yet, just write down 3-10 things you would like to accomplish.

Some sample goals might look like this:

Year 1

- Eliminate all debt except house and car
- Get spending within suggested guidelines in this book
- Completely rest and do what you want 1 day per week

Year 2

- Be positive cash flow each month
- $2,500 in savings at year end
- Take a cheap 1 week vacation

Year 3

- $4,000 in savings by year end
- Set some long term goals (5-10 years) like house purchase or retirement

Now, for each goal, write down exactly what you think you need to do to accomplish that goal in each of the coming years. It is really not that complicated.

This can be your plan for the next several years. Yes, it might change from time to time. Yes, you might not meet all of your goals, but I think you will be surprised how many you will achieve if you just take the time to write them down.

I have attached a few forms in the back of this book to help you get started on your goal planning.

Finally, create a time every year when you can evaluate these goals and your progress. My wife and I do this around New Year's each year. We get out this old piece of paper from many years ago and discuss how we are doing, sometimes discard goals, and sometimes add a new one in. It is a much better way to ring in the New Year than nursing a hangover on New Year's Day!

Now, when putting together your plan, consider the following tips:

1. Control your cash flow and save it

I hate to let you down, but this is the really big secret in getting ahead: Make a bit more than you spend and save it. There it is, that's the big secret. You can either increase your income or reduce your expenses. Either way, it will create a surplus. Save this surplus for many years at a modest rate of return and you will be in good shape.

Albert Einstein called compound inters the eighth wonder of the world. That is, money doubles every seven years if you are getting 10% interest. That is, every seven years, what you had will double. This isn't fancy financial analysis. A simple mutual fund from a major brokerage house like Charles

Schwab, Vanguard, or Fidelity will do. You won't get 10% every year, but the stock market has gone up an average of more than 10% per year over the last forty years. Just put the money in a boring mutual fund and let it grow. Keep an eye on it, but don't watch it every day either. In twenty years, your money will have grown by over 300%.

I heard it said that you are a financial success, or wealthy, when the income off your investments covers your living expenses. Think of that. If you can really be comfortable with very little, you can be a financial success, almost overnight. Of course, you may be living with your mother-in-law and getting around town on a bike, but if this works for you, go for it. If you expect more, you need to save more and spend more time getting to where you want to be. This is why I said that the first step is to set some goals.

Again, it is surprising to me how many people in our society really do not have a clear idea of what they make every month or, even more commonly, what they spend! As a result, it is impossible to plan for their financial destiny.

Be aware of what is coming in and know and control what is going out. Save this over time and you will be a financial success.

2. Do not accumulate debt on high-interest credit cards

Accumulating debt on credit cards is the number one reason why individuals find it necessary to file for bankruptcy. Our advice is never, ever let debt stay on a credit card account for more than sixty days. Essentially, accumulating credit card debt is like taking out a loan at 21%. Very few people would knowingly take out a loan at 21%. Credit card debt needs to be viewed for what it really is; an extremely high interest loan. Even worse, with high-interest rates and low monthly payments the debt never seems to go away. In fact, the bulk of the monthly payment simply goes to pay interest. A recent television news show estimated that it could take as long as thirty-three years to pay off credit card debt by only paying the minimum monthly amount. This is why people feel they can "never get ahead" when they have a large amount of debt on their credit cards.

If the amount of debt on all of your credit cards exceeds two months' pay, you should immediately take steps to remedy the situation as you may very soon be financially "terminal."

3. Do not spend too much on housing

We recommend, as do most financial experts, that individuals not spend more than 30% of their net (take home) pay on their housing. This can be difficult to do especially in areas like Southern California or New York where the cost of housing is quite high. However, it is an extremely good goal or rule of thumb to follow. We commonly see families who are spending 50-60% of their take home pay on housing. Obviously, this cannot be allowed to continue for very long as there is not enough money to cover transportation, insurance, food, etc.

4. Do not overspend on transportation

Experts recommend that not more than 20% of a person's take home pay be spent on transportation. This includes car payments, gasoline, insurance, and repairs. Again, it is very difficult to meet this standard, especially in areas such as California where good, private transportation is still a necessity. However, it is an extremely good goal to meet. Owning an economical car is an ideal way to avoid high transportation costs.

5. Keep your overhead low

It seems as though the goal in the 80's and 90's was to make and spend more money. We see the goal of the new millennium as work smarter, spend less, and feel safer. It is important to take a look at your minimum monthly overhead and know what that number is. If there should be some disruption in your income stream, how would these expenses be met? Obviously, the lower this number, the higher likelihood of financial survival.

6. Create Two Types of Savings

Everyone should consider creating a plan to develop two types of savings.

First, everyone should have six months' worth of net income in a savings or money market account. This money acts as a "safety net" in the event of an extraordinary expenditure or loss of income. Many people also consider this savings account their "self-confidence" money. That is, they are not entirely dependent on their job or others and can walk away from a bad situation with very short notice should they need to.

Second, everyone should consider long-term savings for retirement or a complete catastrophic event. Very few people these days really believe they can rely solely on Social Security when they retire. It is up to each individual to develop some type of savings plan or pension. It is amazing how fast money can compound in this account. For example, saving $200 per week for ten years invested in an account which will turn an average of 10% per year will yield a quarter of a million dollars! The vast majority of our population has ten years of income earning years in front of them. Also, do not forget to contribute the maximum amount allowed for retirement accounts. These investments provide tax deductions and tax-deferred earnings. Retirement accounts may also provide protection from future creditors' claims.

It sometimes is not easy and it takes self-discipline, but the rule is: make savings happen.

7. Act fast if you lose your job

When someone is laid off, they often get a severance package. However, if they don't act fast, the severance package will soon be gone. They start to live on credit cards and are financially ruined a short time thereafter. Also, if you are out of a job for too long, employers are less likely to hire you. The rule is, if you are laid off or lose your job, take a week or so off to rest, but then hit the pavement running!

8. Do not guarantee loans for others

Many people experience financial hardships because they try to help someone else obtain a loan. Very often a default occurs and the person who guaranteed the loan several years earlier (and has maybe even forgotten the loan) now faces financial ruin.

9. Always consider "What If?"

Always have a contingency plan for loss of income. It used to be that jobs in aerospace were "sure bets", meaning those jobs were extremely secure. Recent history has shown us that even sure-bet jobs may not continue forever. Accordingly, a contingency plan must be in place should a sudden loss of income occur. This contingency plan can include appropriate forms of insurance to cover loss of income as well as liability.

Do not fail to provide for adequate insurance coverage. Lawsuits today are an epidemic. Some estimate that one in fifteen people will be the subject of a lawsuit next year. Adequate insurance to provide against such liability is essential.

Be cautious with your investments. Do not necessarily invest in what everyone else believes is a great investment. Consider what will happen if everyone is wrong. The majority is often wrong at market tops. Remember how everyone believed that housing prices would always continue upwards? Be wary of investing in initial public stock offerings and overly-aggressive mutual funds.

10. Spend some time with "success literature"

This last tip is perhaps the most important. The business environment today is nothing short of brutal. Employers are requiring more of their people, taxes have been going up and the economy, especially in California, still seems to have fundamental problems which may not change in the near future.

While this is a dreary picture, it is also a real opportunity for a motivated person.

Our brains are incredible computers. However, they can be "corrupted" with negative data which we all receive on a day to day basis. This negative data can come from the media or from the general negative attitude which so many in our society seem to have. This negative information can corrupt the "data base" in our minds much the way a virus can corrupt the hard drive on our computers.

Accordingly, everyone owes it to themselves to have some type of consistent input of data which is positive. We call this "success" literature. This means books, tapes, and seminars by any of the individuals out there who are lecturing in the success arena. It really does not matter who you choose, whether it be Zig Zigler, Earl Nightingale, or even Anthony Robbins. Many people comment they find this input of positive data from within their own religious faith. It is not so important who you choose to provide you with this positive data. However, it is important that you choose someone with whom you can identify with. Then, you need to make the commitment to listen and allow your brain to be exposed to this positive data on a daily basis.

In counseling numerous individuals with financial problems, we see people develop a negative mind set. This serves to further increase their downward spiral. Success literature will not prevent financial calamity, but may very well serve as an "inoculation" against these negative thoughts and the downward spiral they can lead to.

Applying the above principles to one's own financial life will allow you to have a healthier financial life with significantly less stress and much less likelihood of needing the protection of the Bankruptcy Code.

X. CREDIT REPAIR

Credit repair clinics claim that they can remove bad credit and bankruptcies from your credit report. Do not believe it! Most of these operations are scams. Many clinics simply take your money and perform no valuable service for you.

A bankruptcy filing appears on your credit report from seven to ten years. However, a bankruptcy on your credit report does not necessarily mean financial ruin. Lenders may still qualify you for loans. For example, many banks or savings and loans will qualify people for home loans two years after a bankruptcy.

One way to improve your credit rating after a bankruptcy is by making timely payments on any remaining or new debts. This creates a good payment history which will have a positive effect on your credit rating.

Another way to develop credit after bankruptcy is by re-establishing a credit relationship with a previous creditor. You can do this by paying off any credit cards on which you owe very little prior to the bankruptcy. Credit cards or other debts with zero balances do not need to be listed on your bankruptcy at all. These "zero balance" accounts can many times be used after the bankruptcy proceeding is complete. Obviously, we cannot guarantee that any particular creditor will continue to allow you to have credit with them in the future. Some banks and department stores occasionally learn of the bankruptcy filing even though they were not listed in the schedules. However, we have found from our years of experience that many times this is the best way to re-establish credit accounts.

We have found that many can rehabilitate their financial condition in as short as two years. This usually involves a careful analysis of one's cash flow and a systematic plan to accumulate funds. There are many good books available which discuss this as well, several of which are best sellers. Feel free to contact us and we will send you a list of these books.

Some banks offer "secured" credit cards. The bank provides you with a VISA or MasterCard when you maintain a specified savings account balance with them. In effect, your own funds secure the payment of all charges. This is an excellent way to immediately obtain new credit.

XI. A FAVOR

If you like the simple, basic explanations in this book, do me a favor and pass it around. Yes, I would love to sell many more copies of this book. More importantly, I would be happier if you would simply pass around this book to anyone that you run into that you may believe are having financial problems. I would get more satisfaction in helping to make the financial portion of people's lives better than making money by selling additional copies of the book. That being said, I would appreciate your respect of my copyright. However, letting someone borrow this book and then return it to you would be a great thing for you to do for them financially. Nowadays everyone needs someone on their side, and this book is my way of doing so for you.

XII. CONCLUSION

See, this has really not been too complicated, right?

You can read this book in an hour or two and then spend a similar amount of time developing your remedial plan and then your plan to move forward. These plans can be developed in a long afternoon.

I encourage you to take your first step today on your journey to change and applaud you on your courage to take control of your financial destiny.

APPENDIX A

California Exemptions

The following are the two sets of exemptions that are available to California residents. In California, you can only choose one set. You cannot choose from both. Deciding which set might be best should only be done in consultation with an attorney. Residents of other states should check with a local attorney in their state. A great place to find a qualified attorney is to contact the local bar association and see if they have an attorney referral service. Most larger bar associations have such a service.

EXEMPTIONS - SET NO. 1

1. A HOMESTEAD IN YOUR PRIMARY RESIDENCE

The amount of this exemption is:
   -$75,000 for a single person,
   -$100,000 for a married person OR a head of household,
   -$175,000 for a person 65 years or older OR a disabled person, OR a person 55 years or older with an income of less than $25,000 (or $35,000 if a married couple).

To qualify for the homestead exemption, the property must be the principal residence of the debtor or the debtor's spouse. The Bankruptcy Code now also requires that a person is only entitled to a maximum homestead of $125,000 until such time as they have lived in that state for approximately 3.4 years. (This will obviously only relate to those claiming the larger $175,000 homestead amount.)

The exemption is for equity in the property. For exemption purposes, equity is determined by taking the fair market value of the property and subtracting the value of any consensual liens (mortgages and deeds of trust).

2. MOTOR VEHICLE

The maximum allowed is $2,900 total equity in motor vehicles.

3. HOUSEHOLD FURNISHINGS AND PERSONAL EFFECTS

All of your household furnishings, personal effects, and appliances are free from your creditors' claims so long as they are reasonable and necessary. If you have a household item which has unusually high value (such as an extremely rare antique), it may not be exempt.

4. JEWELRY

The maximum exemption is $7,625 in jewelry, heirlooms, and works of art.

5. HEALTH AIDS

Reasonably necessary health aides are exempt.

6. TOOLS OF THE TRADE

You can exempt up to $7,625 in tools, books, equipment, and one commercial motor vehicle if reasonably necessary and actually used in the exercise of your trade, business, or profession. If both you and your spouse are in a trade, business, or profession, this section specifically allows each of you a $7,625 exemption. This may be used to exempt a vehicle so long as it is used for business purposes, up to $4,850.

7. BUILDING MATERIALS

Materials that are to be used to repair or improve your residence are exempt up to $3,050.

8. LIFE INSURANCE

A policy with no cash value is totally exempt. The maximum exemption for the cash value of a policy is $12,200 or $24,400 if you are married. Benefits from matured life insurance or annuity policies are exempt to the extent reasonably necessary for the support of the debtor and his or her spouse or dependents.

9. DISABILITY, UNEMPLOYMENT, AND HEALTH INSURANCE BENEFITS

Payments from these types of insurance are exempt with no dollar limit.

10. PERSONAL INJURY CLAIMS

A lawsuit, or the right to sue someone, is an asset in the eyes of the law. When a personal injury cause of action (the right to sue) has not yet been reduced to a judgment and paid, the entire claim is exempt. When money has been paid as a result of a personal injury accident, the money is exempt, but only to the extent that it is reasonably necessary for the support of you and your dependents. If the award or settlement is payable in installments, each payment is exempt except to the extent that the same amount of earnings would be subject to wage garnishment.

11. WRONGFUL DEATH CLAIMS

A wrongful death claim is exempt to the same extent as a personal injury claim.

12. WORKERS' COMPENSATION CLAIMS AND AWARDS

A workers' compensation claim and award is completely exempt without limitation.

13. PUBLIC RETIREMENT BENEFITS

All amounts held for your retirement by a "public entity" are exempt without limitation. "Public entities" are governmental bodies as well as public corporations.

14. PRIVATE RETIREMENT BENEFITS

Benefits payable or paid under private retirement accounts, union retirement plans, and profit-sharing plans designed and used for retirement purposes are exempt in an unlimited amount. This section is intended to exempt only retirement plans established or maintained by private employers or employee organizations, such as unions, not arrangements by individuals to use specified assets for retirement purposes. Funds in self-employment retirement plans and individual retirement annuities and accounts (including IRAs) may be exempt if designed and used principally for retirement purposes. To determine whether an IRA has been designed and used principally for retirement, many factors are relevant including (1) the purpose of any withdrawals from the IRA, (2) whether applicable withdrawal procedures were followed, (3) the frequency of withdrawals, (4) whether the IRA was being used to shield funds from creditors or the court, and (5) whether withdrawals were inconsistent with the purpose of the IRA (to be used for long-term retirement).

Amounts in self-employment retirement plans and IRAs are subject to the further limitation that they are exempt only to the extent necessary for the support of the debtor (and his or her spouse and dependents) at the time of retirement, taking into account all of the resources likely to be available to the debtor when he or she retires. The court is to take into account all resources that are likely to be available for the support of the debtor when the debtor retires.

NOTE: The U.S. Supreme Court has held that any retirement plan which is ERISA qualified or contains a "spendthrift" provision can be kept by a person filing bankruptcy, regardless of the amount in the plan.

ALSO NOTE: Under current law, retirement funds in an account exempt from taxation under IRC §§401, 403, 408, 408A, 414, 457, or 501(a) are exempt irrespective of their treatment under the above state exemption. This new exemption includes IRA accounts up to a maximum of $1,245,475 (as of 4/1/13), although this amount may be increased "if the interests of justice so require."

15. PRE-PETITION WAGES

Wages earned 30 days prior to the bankruptcy are partially exempt. This exemption protects 75 percent of the amount you received during this period. If these wages were subject to garnishment, all of these funds are exempt. (Of course, all wages you receive after the bankruptcy is filed are free of creditors' claims).

16. PRISONER'S FUND

The maximum exemption is $1,525.

17. CHARITABLE AID, STUDENT LOANS, AND RELOCATION BENEFITS

Any funds received for these purposes are exempt.

18. CEMETERY PLOT

Any cemetery plot you own is exempt.

19. DEPOSIT ACCOUNTS

If a bank account can be shown to receive Social Security payments by direct deposit, it is protected up to $3,050 for an individual and up to $4,575 for a couple.

EXEMPTIONS - SET NO. 2

1. REAL PROPERTY

A $25,575 exemption in real property (including a mobile home) is allowed if used as a primary residence or burial plot.

2. WILD CARD

We call this exemption the "wild card" because it can exempt $1,350, plus any unused portion of the $25,575 exemption listed in paragraph number 1 above, in any asset. In other words, if you do not claim an exemption in a residence, you have a $26,925 exemption that you can claim in any assets. This can be used to protect cash, savings accounts, vehicles, or just about any other asset you may own.

3. MOTOR VEHICLE

The maximum allowed is $5,100 in one or more motor vehicles.

4. HOUSEHOLD FURNISHINGS AND PERSONAL EFFECTS

An unlimited exemption is allowed in household furnishings, household goods, wearing apparel, appliances, books, animals, crops, or musical instruments, which are held primarily for personal, family, or household use, so long as no single item is worth more than $600.

5. JEWELRY

The maximum exemption is $1,525 in jewelry held primarily for personal, family, or household use.

6. TOOLS OF THE TRADE

A $7,625 exemption is allowed for professional books or tools of your trade.

7. LIFE INSURANCE

An exemption is allowed in any unmatured life insurance policy with no cash value. If the policy has cash value, $13,675 is exempt.

8. HEALTH AIDS

An unlimited amount is allowed for health aids.

9. BENEFITS PAYMENTS

A total exemption is allowed for social security benefits, unemployment compensation, veteran's, disability, or unemployment benefits. Alimony or support payments are also exempt, but only to the extent that they are reasonably necessary for your support and support of any dependents.

10. PENSION PLANS

An exemption is allowed for any payment under a stock, bonus, pension, profit-sharing, annuity, or similar plan on account of illness, death, disability, age, or length of service, to the extent reasonably necessary for the support of the debtor, his or her spouse and any dependents. This exemption applies to IRA accounts which are exempt to the extent required for the debtor's support at retirement. Courts have ruled that what is reasonably necessary for the support of the debtor should be sufficient to sustain basic needs, and not related to the debtor's former status in society or lifestyle to which he or she is accustomed.

NOTE: The U.S. Supreme Court has held that any retirement plan which is ERISA qualified or contains a "spendthrift" provision can be kept by a person filing bankruptcy regardless of the amount in the plan. If you believe you have these types of plans, you should find out whether they meet this requirement before your bankruptcy is filed.

ALSO NOTE: Retirement funds in an account exempt from taxation under IRC §§401, 403, 408, 408A, 414, 457, or 501(a) are exempt irrespective of their treatment under the above state exemption. This new exemption includes IRA accounts up to a maximum of $1,245,475 (as of 4/1/13), although this amount may be increased "if the interests of justice so require."

11. MISCELLANEOUS PAYMENTS

Exemptions are allowed for (1) any payments under a crime victims' reparation law, and (2) any payments on account of the wrongful death of a person of whom the debtor was a dependent or on account of a life insurance contract, but only to the extent reasonably necessary for the support of the debtor and his or her dependents.

12. PERSONAL INJURY CLAIMS

Any payment on account of a personal injury lawsuit is exempt up to $24,060. Compensation for loss of future earnings is exempt to the extent reasonably necessary for your support or the support of your dependents.

APPENDIX B

Goal Worksheets

Goal # _____

_____

_____

_____

_____

_____

Things That Need to be Done to Achieve Goal & Approximate Completion Date

Task	Date

Goal # _____

_____

_____

_____

_____

_____

Things That Need to be Done to Achieve Goal & Approximate
Completion Date

Task	Date

Goal # _____

_____

_____

_____

_____

_____

Things That Need to be Done to Achieve Goal & Approximate Completion Date

Task	Date

Goal # _____

_____
_____
_____
_____
_____

Things That Need to be Done to Achieve Goal & Approximate
Completion Date

Task   Date

_____   _____
_____   _____
_____   _____
_____   _____
_____   _____
_____   _____
_____   _____
_____   _____

www.ingramcontent.com/pod-product-compliance
Lightning Source LLC
Chambersburg PA
CBHW060642210326
41520CB00010B/1707